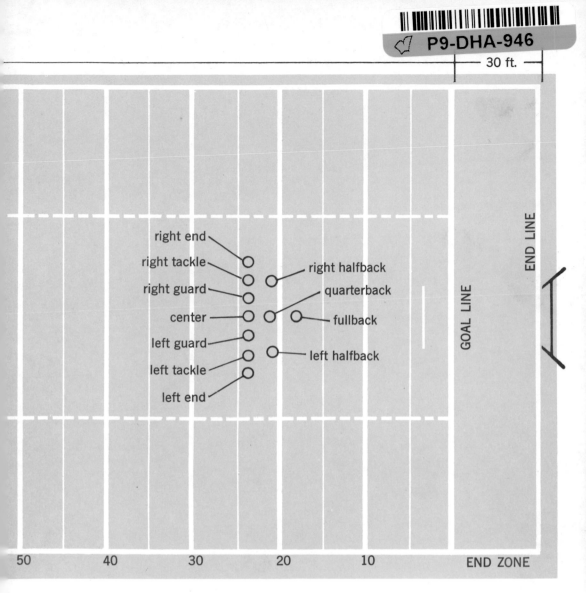

30 ft.

right end
right tackle
right guard
center
left guard
left tackle
left end

right halfback
quarterback
fullback
left halfback

GOAL LINE

END LINE

50   40   30   20   10   END ZONE

On a professional field, the goalposts are set up on the goal lines, instead of the end lines, and the posts are closer together.

The playing area is marked off with white lines every five yards. These lines, which are made by spreading powdered lime, make the field look like a huge griddle. This is why the field is sometimes called the "gridiron."

Two dotted lines, also made with powdered lime, run from goal line to goal line. They are called the inbounds lines. The ball must always be put into play between these lines.

VINCE LOMBARDI
FOOTBALL LEGEND

★ ★ ★ ★ ★ ★ ★ ★ ★ ★

BY LES ETTER

ILLUSTRATED BY HERMAN VESTAL

GARRARD PUBLISHING COMPANY
CHAMPAIGN, ILLINOIS

To my wife Jean, for all her help.

Library of Congress Cataloging in Publication Data

Etter, Les.
    Vince Lombardi: football legend.

    SUMMARY: A brief biography of the football coach
who turned Wisconsin's Green Bay Packers into a
virtually unbeatable team.

    1. Lombardi, Vince—Juvenile literature. 2. Foot-
ball—Juvenile literature. 3. Football coaching—
Juvenile literature. [1. Lombardi, Vince. 2. Foot-
ball—Biography] I. Vestal, Herman, B., illus.
II. Title.
GV939.L6E88   796.33′2′0924 [B] [92]   74–18076
ISBN 0–8116–6670–0

Photo credits:

United Press International: pp. 24, 56, 62 (bottom), 63,
    73, 78 (both), 82, 90, 91, 95
Wide World: pp. 3, 42–43, 62 (top)

Contents

1. Run to Daylight!

A group of boys was playing football behind an old warehouse in Brooklyn, New York. It was a fall afternoon in the middle 1920s, and the game was like many others being played all over the city that day.

Each side had eleven players, more or less. None of them wore helmets or shoulder pads although the ground was bare and stony. Such fancy trimmings were not for this part of Brooklyn. They were for rich kids, or older high school teams.

"Who's winning?" demanded a newcomer on the sideline.

"It's tied at three touchdowns apiece," replied a small boy excitedly. "It's the Eagles' ball, but we'll lick 'em! Come on, Giants! Let's go Vinnie!"

The center snapped the ball. It struck the hands of a halfback and bounded away.

"Fumble!" Players on both teams scrambled after the lopsided old pigskin.

A stocky, black-haired boy reached it first with a reckless dive. "Atta way, Lombardi!" yelled the fans. "Go get 'em, Vin!"

The referee, an older boy, called out: "Giants' ball, first and ten. Hurry it up— time for only three more plays!"

A babble of shrill voices broke out around the quarterback. "Hit center!" cried one player. "Throw a long pass!" urged another. Someone else wanted an end run. The quarterback looked rattled.

6

Thirteen-year-old Vince Lombardi's hand shot up. "Cut out the chatter!" he snapped. "Nobody can pass that old balloon." He whispered to the quarterback, "I'll take it on an off-tackle smash." He glanced around. "Give me some interference!" he ordered.

The other players nodded. Vinnie always seemed to know what to do. He was small for his age, but he was tough and strong.

"Signals!" shouted the quarterback.

Vince Lombardi crouched in the fullback spot. He took the snapback and raced to his right. There was a wild mix-up as the defenders charged in. His path was blocked, and the sideline was too close for a run around end.

Then Vince's keen eyes saw a gap in the line. "Run to daylight!" he panted to himself. He cut back sharply the way Hinkey Haines of the New York Giants did at the Polo Grounds.

Daylight loomed ahead—all the way to the goal line.

"Touchdown!" shouted his teammates. "Yea, Lombardi!"

There were no goal posts on that hard ground—so there were no extra points to kick. Only touchdowns counted. The Giants won, four touchdowns to three.

Vince felt a bloody scratch on his face and grinned. How he loved to win at football! He'd played it in the streets and on the sandlots ever since he could remember. At first, the older kids had cried, "Beat it, runt," when he tried to join them. Now they begged him to play on their side.

As the players left the field, the referee ran to catch up with Vince. "How come you know so much about football?" he asked. "You should be the quarterback."

"Not me," Vince replied. "I like to hit the line."

"Yeah—but where'd you learn so much about plays?"

"I go to the Polo Grounds to watch the Giants every chance I get," said Vince. "They're my favorite team. I read the sport pages, and I study those charts in the Sunday papers. You know—where coaches like Knute Rockne of Notre Dame explain their best plays."

"Is that where you learned about that off-tackle play?"

"No. That's the Giants best groundgainer," Vince explained. "I watched them beat the Yellow Jackets with it. Their best halfback, Hinkey Haines, got smeared with it at first. He kept his head down and ran into a pile-up. Then everybody started yelling, 'Run to daylight! Run to daylight!' They meant he should run where the hole was—not where it was supposed to be!"

"You'll make a high school quarterback

some day," said the referee. "You'll have to grow a lot though."

Vince's dark eyes flashed. His size was a sore point with him. "Don't you worry about me!" he replied sharply. "I can take care of myself!"

"Sure you can—but get the chip off your shoulder," said the referee. "See you later."

It was almost dark when Vince reached the street where the Lombardis lived in a

two-story house. The lights were on, and Vince hurried even faster.

Papa always insisted that the whole family be on time for meals. To be late meant trouble. He glanced at his torn shirt and felt the scratch on his cheek again. Mama wouldn't like that, but he shrugged. Papa would ignore scratches like that. They were only "little hurts," he said.

Vince forgot these things as he charged

through the door. His brothers and sisters would be waiting to hear about the game.

"We won—we're champs of the block!" he shouted as he dashed inside. "Run to daylight!"

Vince Lombardi would echo these words many times in the exciting years ahead. One day he would even write a book with that title: *Run to Daylight!*

2. "My Brother Can Lick Your Father!"

Vincent Thomas Lombardi was born in the Sheepshead Bay section of Brooklyn, June 11, 1913. He was the oldest of five children born to Henry and Matilda Izzo Lombardi. He had two brothers, Harold and Joe, and two sisters, Madeline and Claire.

His father came from Italy, and his mother was born in America. The family name means "conquering longbeard." It was the name of an ancient German tribe that settled in northern Italy many centuries ago.

Vince's parents were deeply religious and quite strict with their children. Following an

13

Italian custom, Mr. Lombardi placed his oldest son in charge of the other children. It was Vince's duty to see that his father's orders were carried out exactly as they were given.

Vince tried to be fair, but he carefully obeyed his father. His brothers and sisters learned he would stand for no nonsense. If they failed in their tasks, Vince soon set them straight. They came to look up to, and depend upon, him.

But sometimes Vince became careless, too. Once his father took time off from his job as a wholesale meat dealer to tear down an old barn behind their house. School was closed for the summer, so Vince had to help.

The job seemed simple enough. Mr. Lombardi removed the boards from the barn and handed them to Vince. "Pull out the nails and pile the boards in three separate stacks according to length," he said.

But the day was hot, and Vince soon grew tired. It was easier to pile the boards together, the longer ones on top. His father, busy inside the barn, didn't see him.

As the stack grew higher, little Harold Lombardi began to play on it. "Get down before you fall," warned Vince. But Harold only climbed higher. Suddenly the uneven stack toppled over, pinning the boy beneath it.

Harold wasn't badly hurt, but Mr. Lombardi was furious. "If you'd piled those boards as I told you to, this wouldn't have happened," he shouted.

Vince started to speak, but his father said shortly, "No excuses! Now get busy and do the job right."

It took a long time to pile the boards over again. When he finished, Vince was very tired. His hands were blistered and bleeding. But his father was satisfied. Then

Mr. Lombardi saw his son wince as he picked the slivers from his hands.

"Don't mind a few slivers, Vin," his father said. "They're nothing. The important thing is to do the job right—hurt is only in your mind." Vince never forgot his father's words.

Although Mr. Lombardi was often gruff with him, Vince understood his father's sternness and hot temper. For Vince was hot-tempered too.

Sometimes that temper got him into trouble with other kids. The streets of Brooklyn were no place for a timid boy, and Vince soon learned to use his fists well. His brothers and sisters were proud of his fighting ability.

Once when the younger Lombardis were quarreling with the kids next door, one of their neighbors shouted, "My father can lick your father!"

Quick as a flash, little Joe Lombardi replied, "Oh, yeah? And my brother can lick your father!"

In school Vince was a good student, and his name was often on the class honor roll. He became an altar boy in his church, and he began to think of becoming a priest.

By the time he was seventeen, Vince had made up his mind. He entered Brooklyn's Cathedral Preparatory Seminary to study for the priesthood. He was so well liked by his fellow students that he was elected president of his class the second semester.

Cathedral Prep had no football squad, but it did have basketball and baseball teams. Vince played on both teams, and he liked Coach John "Jocko" Crane.

Crane stressed the value of teamwork. "A team that plays well together usually can beat one that depends upon an individual star. No one player can do it all alone."

During the football season, Vince still played on the sandlots. He was not a star, but he loved football and he held his own in the rough, hard play.

After a couple of semesters, Vince reached a turning point in his life. His grades were still high, but he decided not to become a priest.

The next fall he entered Saint Francis Prep, another Brooklyn high school, to take a college preparatory course. He didn't have any money for tuition, but he was determined to go to college.

Vince had a bright idea. Perhaps he could put his sandlot football experience to good use. Saint Francis had a fine football team. If he could win a place on it and keep up his grades, he might earn a college scholarship. He knew that many athletes got their college educations that way. It was worth giving it a try.

Harry Kane, the Saint Francis coach, was impressed by Vince's fire and ambition. He had taught a number of boys who later became fine college players.

But Kane knew that Vince had only sandlot experience. He would have a lot to learn. "Unless you give me one hundred percent effort," he warned, "you'd better stick to the sandlots!"

Eagerly Vince agreed, and he soon found that Kane was an excellent teacher. He was a hard driver, but he had sound reasons for everything he did.

"Blocking and tackling—that's football!" Kane said. "There's no greater satisfaction than to do them right."

Vince improved steadily. By his senior season of 1932, he was fullback on the All-Metropolitan Catholic High School team. The scholarship offers came, and he chose one from Fordham University.

20

Fordham was a fine academic school, and its football team, called the Rams, was among the best in the country. Even more important to Vince, Jim Crowley was the head coach.

Crowley had been a member of the famous Four Horsemen backfield under Knute Rockne at Notre Dame. Every boy in America knew about them. He had been nicknamed "Sleepy Jim" as a player, but there was nothing sleepy about his coaching. His Michigan State teams were big winners before he came East to Fordham.

Vince looked forward to playing for Crowley. He had his scholarship. Now he was determined to make good all the way.

3. Seven Blocks of Granite

An assistant coach at Fordham University was looking over the incoming freshman football players the first day of practice in 1933.

When he came to a short, dark-haired boy, he was not impressed. "Too small," he thought. But he asked, "Name and position, son?"

"Lombardi—I'm a lineman," replied Vince quickly. He knew he wasn't big enough for a college fullback, or fast enough for a halfback. He felt his best chance was in the line.

22

The assistant grinned. "A lineman, huh?" he said. Fordham's varsity line was one of the best in the country. The players were big and tough. All of them weighed well above two hundred pounds. Surely this kid didn't think he could break into a lineup like that.

"Okay," said the coach. "Take your stance. We'll see."

Vince crouched down. Without warning the man lunged at him and knocked him backward. Vince was angry as he picked himself up.

"Want to try it again?" the coach challenged.

Vince nodded. This time he was ready. Before the coach could move, Vince drove into him with all his strength. The assistant's cap flew off. He hit the ground with a thump.

Vince's fists were clenched as he waited

for the coach to get up. The coach only smiled. "Okay, Lombardi," he said. "You'll do."

The next fall Vince played only part-time on the varsity. But in 1935, he played right guard on the Rams' famous "Seven Blocks of Granite" line. He was the lightest man on it at 172 pounds.

Vince tried hard to overcome this handicap with extra hustle and hard blocking.

Vince (third from left) played right guard on the Fordham "Seven Blocks of Granite" line.

Still Coach Crowley seemed to drive him harder than the other players.

One day Crowley's whistle blasted. "Where are those famous Blocks of Granite I've been reading about?" he demanded. "The rocks must be in your feet! Move!"

After another play he shouted, "Lombardi —lead the play—don't foul it up! Block that tackle out, not in!"

Vince staggered up. An elbow had caught his chin. His lips were bloody. He was so tired he could hardly stand. The sun was setting behind the old wooden bleachers on Fordham Field. Practice was almost over— but not quite.

"Same play!" cried the coach. "Run it right this time, Lombardi, unless you want to stay here all night."

Vince bowled over the defensive tackle. "Not good, but better!" snorted Crowley. "Everybody take five laps around the field."

Vince jogged beside his buddy, Andy Palau, the Rams' quarterback. "Coach reminds me of my father," he said. "I couldn't do anything right for him either."

"That's because they both want you to do your best all the time," replied Palau. "Coach Crowley rides us because we've got the hardest schedule in the country. Who else meets Pittsburgh, Georgia, Saint Mary's, Texas, and Purdue—all in one season? We've got to be tough."

Vince played in many hard games as first-string right guard in 1935–36. But the 1936 Pittsburgh game was the hardest of all.

The Pitt Panthers were Fordham's greatest rivals in the East. They fought to three scoreless ties in 1935, 1936, and 1937. These were hard, rough contests, and Vince played 60 minutes in the first two.

In the '36 contest, Vince had to block tough Tony Matisi, the Panthers' 220-pound

All-American tackle. Sometimes he and Andy Palau had to double-team block Matisi. But Andy's 165 pounds didn't help much.

Every time Vince charged, Tony's big forearm raked across his mouth. Vince was dazed and bleeding by the time Pitt began a final drive toward the Fordham goal. The Panthers charged to the five-yard line. With fourth down coming up, the ball was on the Rams' two.

The play was called. Dimly Vince saw the Pitt blockers swarming toward him. He dove desperately beneath their pounding legs. He was barely conscious as his excited teammates hauled him from the bottom of the pile-up.

"Great going, Vince!" someone shouted in his ear. "You stopped 'em on the one!"

When the game ended, the team doctor took Vince into the Polo Grounds dressing room and put 30 stitches in his mouth. Afterward Vince said, "I thought of my father's words several times that afternoon. The hurt was in my mind, all right, but I had a mighty sore mouth, too."

Vince Lombardi's last game as a Fordham senior in 1936 was one of his best. It also was one of his biggest disappointments.

Fordham was unbeaten going into its final contest, against New York University. The NYU Violets hadn't won a game all season. Everyone expected an easy Fordham victory.

If the Rams won, they were almost sure to be invited to play in the Rose Bowl against the University of Washington, the Pacific Coast champion.

But Coach Crowley was worried; the team was too cocky. The Rams thought the game would be a runaway—that is, all but Vince Lombardi.

When the game began, Vince was all over

the field. He blocked and tackled. He raged at his teammates, trying to wake them up. But before the stunned Rams knew what had happened, NYU had scored a touchdown. The Rams lost the game, 7–6, and with it the Rose Bowl bid.

Afterward, Coach Crowley told reporters, "Lombardi was the only man who played up to form. He's been our most underrated player all season. I'm mighty proud of him."

The praise didn't help Vince. Nothing could take away the hurt of losing. He didn't speak to anyone on the campus for days. He hated to face defeat, and his feelings never changed. Years later he said, "Winning isn't everything. It's the only thing."

4. High School Coach

Vince graduated from Fordham University with a business degree in 1937. He had been on the dean's list for four years as an honor student.

Now he decided to study law. He began to take courses in night school at Fordham. To pay his way, he worked days for a finance company. Sometimes he earned extra money playing football for a minor league team called the Brooklyn Eagles. But he was too small to become a regular pro player.

Vince became worried. He was not earning much, and a law course was expensive. There was a depression in America, and good jobs were scarce.

One day in 1939 Vince received a call from his college friend Andy Palau. Andy was head coach at Saint Cecelia High School in Englewood, New Jersey. He wanted Vince to become his assistant.

Vince didn't want to give up his law course, but he loved football. Then Andy told him he could earn enough to keep up his studies. That settled it. He took the job.

Besides football, he had to coach basketball and baseball and teach physics, chemistry, math, and Latin.

Vince hadn't played much basketball, but Andy had been a Fordham star. He gave Vince a "crash course" in the sport. Vince learned so well that by 1945 his team became state parochial school champion.

In 1942 Andy went to Fordham to coach the freshmen, and Vince Lombardi became the head coach at Saint Cecelia. His football teams were winners from the start. Vince was the first football coach in New Jersey to teach the T-formation. He taught the "Saints" the same strong blocking and tackling he had learned at Fordham.

"We learned a lot of football from Coach Lombardi," one of the Saints said. "It was the same in the classroom. He explained things so simply that if you listened you understood. If you didn't listen, he might bounce a piece of chalk off your head."

One of his players was Joe Lombardi, who had reached high school age. Vince loved his younger brother, but he treated him just as he treated every other player. Joe worked hard to improve himself, and when Vince saw that he had real ability, he drove him even harder.

The Saints had no blocking sleds or dummies, so Vince made his players line up before each scrimmage to block him. Poor Joe was always first in line.

Vince wore no pads—only shorts, a T-shirt, and a baseball cap. As Joe crouched before him, his brother would growl, "Okay! Hit me on the three count! One—two—"

Each time Joe was knocked sprawling. It took him a long time, but he finally figured out why Vince outcharged him. One day he didn't wait for the full three count. Instead he charged just after Vince shouted "two!" This time his big brother went tumbling backward.

Vince sprang up and grabbed Joe's hand. "Good boy!" he shouted. "You figured it out for yourself. I could have told you, but this way you'll remember."

Saint Cecelia was a small school. The Saints often faced much heavier squads. But

Vince's teams were quick, and they played heads-up football.

Sometimes larger teams tried to beat the Saints by rough play. In one game Joe Lombardi and his teammates were bruised and bleeding by halftime. In the locker room they spoke angrily of revenge in the second half.

"I'm going to belt their right tackle," cried one player. "He gave me a knee or an elbow every time I blocked him."

Vince jumped up and called for silence. He looked at the players sternly.

"The first man who tries any rough stuff comes out of the game!" he snapped. "My teams don't play dirty football."

The Saints finally won. As they left the field, one of the players shouted, "Hey, look at coach! He's really steaming!"

They saw Vince catch up with the rival coach in front of the other team's dressing-room door. Vince's fists were clenched, and his head bobbed angrily as he spoke.

The Saint Cecelia players knew their coach. "I'll bet they don't try that on us again," said one. They didn't.

Vince was tough, but he could be understanding, too. Once a young halfback, playing his first game, fumbled twice.

The subs on the bench watched Coach Lombardi closely. They saw his eyes blink rapidly behind his glasses—a sure sign he was upset. They waited for him to explode.

The kid fumbled again. This time the Saints lost the ball.

Vince waved the unlucky player to him. Then he saw the tears in the frightened boy's eyes. Suddenly he smiled. "What's the matter, son?" he asked. "Put some resin on your hands and get back out there."

But Vince seldom relaxed in practice. These sessions were highly organized to make every minute count. Players had to be on the field before the coach blew his whistle. Latecomers would be greeted with an angry order.

"Take four laps around the field," Vince would shout. "Maybe that'll wake you up!"

During scrimmages Vince would stalk the sidelines. Even with his thick glasses his vision was poor. But he always knew what was happening on the field. A shoddy block or tackle would bring an instant roar. "You missed that block," he'd shout. "Four laps after practice—and sprint the last 50 yards!"

Training rules were just as strict. One was that players must be in bed by ten o'clock the night before a game. Once he came home after ten to find Joe Lombardi scrubbing the kitchen floor.

"Mom's having a party tomorrow," Joe explained hastily.

"You should have started earlier," said

Vince. "You don't play tomorrow." And he didn't.

Joe became All-Metropolitan guard, and Vince went to the All-Metro banquet with him. He had never attended the party before. It was his way of showing Joe how proud he was of him.

When Vince married his college sweetheart, Marie Planitz, in 1940, he began to think seriously of the future. By now he felt that coaching was his lifework, and he gave up his law studies to give full time to it.

By 1946 the Saints had won 39 of 51 games under Vince, tied 5 and lost 7. Their record included a 25-game winning streak. Vince began to receive coaching offers from larger high schools. But he wanted to become a college coach.

When Fordham asked him to take over the freshman squad, he accepted eagerly.

5. Vince Goes to West Point

Vince Lombardi coached the freshman team to an unbeaten season in 1947, his first year at Fordham. He was moved up to the varsity staff the next fall.

At first Vince was happy at Fordham because he was very fond of the university. He once had dreamed of becoming head coach there. But after two seasons, that prospect looked dim. Ed Danowski, a former Rams star, was doing well at that post.

Vince became restless. He and his wife, Marie, were raising a family. He needed a better job and more money.

40

Late in 1948 Vince got an unexpected break. Colonel Earl "Red" Blaik, coach at the United States Military Academy at West Point, New York, needed an assistant. He wanted someone to take charge of the Army offense.

Tim Cohane, a New York sportswriter, had known Vince since he had played on the Seven Blocks of Granite. Cohane suggested Vince's name to Blaik.

After talking with Vince several times, the Army coach told him: "I think you've got the spark and drive we need."

Vince joined the Army staff for the 1949 season and moved his family to West Point. He plunged into his new job with the same energy he had shown at Saint Cecelia and Fordham.

Soon, however, his temper and impatience got him into trouble. He shouted as angrily at the older cadets as he had at his high school players. Once when a cadet missed a block in practice, Vince bellowed, "That's the worst block I ever saw! Get out of my sight!"

Later Colonel Blaik spoke to his hot-tempered aide. "Vince," he said quietly, "we just don't do things that way at West Point."

Vince apologized. He tried harder than ever to control his temper. He didn't always succeed, but the players understood. They

knew he often became impatient because he was trying so hard to make Army the best team in the land.

As the cadets learned from Vince, he learned from Blaik. "The most important thing that ever happened to me in football," he said later, "was the chance to coach under Colonel Blaik. He molded my whole approach to the game."

Vince's natural talent for teaching football increased rapidly under the colonel. He

Assistant Coach Vince Lombardi watches as cadets on the Army team work out at the U.S. Military Academy at West Point.

often repeated one of Blaik's favorite sayings to his players. "Football is a game of inches," he'd tell them.

After a close scrimmage play, he'd rush to the spot where the ball was downed. "It's close, but you made it!" he'd cry. "Just remember—an Army team must never lose a first down, or a touchdown, by inches! Keep driving until the whistle!"

Blaik also demanded perfect downfield blocking. As the ball was snapped in practice, Vince would dash along the sideline. "Block—block—block!" he'd shout. "Don't stop with the first one. Get down the field!"

Army was one of the first teams to use movies to study its own mistakes and those of its rivals. Once Coach Blaik estimated that he and Vince had spent almost four thousand hours in five years watching game films. Vince became a firm believer in this method of scouting.

One day they were studying films of their next opponent. The team had an All-American tackle. "Look at the way he uses his hands," Vince pointed out. "No wonder other teams keep away from his side of the line!"

"Run that last quarter again," said Colonel Blaik. "This time watch how high he charges. We'll go for his legs."

Vince protested. "But nobody's been able to stop him yet."

"Always attack an opponent's strength," replied Blaik. "Control his strongest point and you win. I believe we can handle that tackle."

Army won. Vince never forgot Blaik's advice, and he used it often in his future career.

The Army coach gave Vince another duty. He was placed in charge of grading players on their performances in games. Sid Gillman,

who had preceded Vince at West Point, had
started this practice, and Vince carried it on
efficiently. The grades were posted for all
the players to see.

After five years of handling the Army
attack, Vince Lombardi was offered a new
challenge. The New York Giants of the
National Football League (NFL) brought
in a new head coach, Jim Lee Howell. He
needed someone to direct the Giants' offense.

Jim Lee had often watched Army in ac-
tion, and he admired Vince's sound methods.

Vince became Howell's assistant. This was
another step upward in Vince's career. He
looked forward eagerly to the 1954 season.

6. Vince Joins the Giants

"You're our left halfback," Vince told Frank Gifford as the New York Giants opened their 1954 training camp.

Gifford was delighted. He'd been a fine triple-threat back at the University of Southern California before the Giants drafted him in 1953. But he'd spent most of his rookie season on defense.

Vince had studied the 1953 Giants on film. One bright spot had been Gifford's play the few times he'd been used on offense. The way he ran, passed, and caught passes gave Vince an idea.

He outlined his plan during a chalk talk, using X's and O's on the blackboard. "This is our new pass-option play," he said. "It starts the same as our sweep. Gifford will run wide on the play. If the defense comes up to meet him, the flanker and end will fake blocks and go downfield as receivers. If it lays back, the flanker and end will go down as blockers."

The play added deception to the Giants' attack. Opposing teams, used to the Giants' old steam-roller tactics, were baffled.

Vince helped solve another problem for the Giants. Charlie Conerly, the veteran quarterback, was tackled behind the line so many times in 1953 that he decided to retire.

Jim Lee Howell talked him out of it. He promised Charlie more pass protection. Vince saw that he got it. And Jim Lee found good ends to receive Charlie's passes. Vince told Conerly, "We'll drop the guards back and

use another halfback to block for you. With Gifford running the option, the defense won't rush in so fast."

"That should help," agreed Conerly.

It did help, and the Giants looked better. They began to win. New York fans came out to watch them again.

But Vince had a personal problem, too. Some of the veterans resented taking orders from a former college assistant coach. They felt they knew more than he did. But Vince didn't lose his temper. When he made mistakes he admitted them and then asked the players' help.

"We learned to respect Vince," one player said. "We saw how much he wanted to win, and he wasn't above asking our advice."

As Vince became accepted by the squad, the veterans sometimes played jokes on him. Once he found an old photo of the Seven Blocks of Granite on the locker-room wall.

"Hey, Vince," someone shouted. "You guys look like seven bullfrogs in that old-fashioned stance!" Vince joined in the laughter.

As the NFL season continued, Frank Gifford ran and passed for solid gains and touchdowns. Conerly, too, bounced back. He completed 103 passes, 17 of them for touchdowns.

When the Giants finished third in the NFL East, Jim Lee said to Vince. "We've got a good start. We're on our way."

But Lombardi wasn't satisfied. "Only first place counts," he muttered to himself.

The Giants future seemed brighter in 1955. Then disaster struck. They lost four of their first five games. Howell tried to resign, but the club wouldn't let him.

Things grew worse until Vince and another assistant, Ed Kolman, had an idea. "Why not try double-team blocking with our running plays?" they asked each other.

"Every T-team in the league brush blocks these days," said Lombardi, "and they all use one-on-one blocking." He meant that offensive linemen just checked the defense long enough to let the runner slip by. And one-on-one blocking pitted one blocker against one defender.

"We'll surprise them," Vince said with a grin. "No one player in the league can handle two blockers. It'll be something different."

Coach Howell agreed, and two double-team plays were quickly put in the Giants' offense. One sent Gifford between tackle and end. Alex Webster, the right halfback, hit a similar hole on the other side of the line.

The new plays helped the Giants win four of their final games. They jumped from last to third place to end the season.

Before the '56 season opened, Howell had drafted a pair of prize college rookies. They were Sam Huff, an All-American tackle from West Virginia, and Don Chandler of Florida, the nation's best college punter.

Although he weighed 235 pounds, Huff was shocked when he overheard one assistant coach ask another, "What about Huff? He's too small for a pro tackle and too slow for a guard."

"Yeah," agreed the other. "And we've already got three good linebackers."

Huff was upset. At the same time Chandler became unhappy because of a shoulder injury. He doubted if punting ability alone could keep him on the squad.

The two rookies decided to go home. They arrived at the airport to learn their plane was late. Meanwhile someone told Vince of their decision. As the boys stood near the door waiting, they were surprised to see a station wagon skid to a stop at the terminal entrance.

Vince leaped out to face them. "You fellows may not make this club," he roared, "but nobody quits on me!"

"If that plane had been on time," Huff said later, "we'd have been on it. That's how close we came to missing out with the Giants." Both became All-Pro choices in coming seasons.

Vince's offense helped the Giants gain the

lead in the East late in 1956. New York began to close in on the division title with a
6–2–1 record.

Now the Giants faced Washington, a team
that had beaten them once. The Redskins
could blast them out of the lead.

Vince Lombardi and Charlie Conerly stood
on the sideline early in the first quarter.
Vince grabbed Conerly's arm. "That middle
linebacker is an eager beaver," he said.
"He tries to make every tackle. We can
trap him and send Gifford through the hole.
If he waits, we'll double-team him."

The strategy worked. The Giants' right
guard checked the linebacker. The left
guard hit the Redskin from the side.

Gifford had a great day. He scored three
touchdowns and passed for another, and the
Giants won. Although they split their next
two contests, they reached the NFL play-off
against the Chicago Bears.

A sneaker-clad Giant halfback lunges over the line for a touchdown in the 1956 championship game against the Chicago Bears.

The Giants defeated the Bears 47–7 in ice-coated Yankee Stadium. It was not a fair test as the Giants wore sneakers to gain a solid footing while their rivals skidded helplessly on the ice. But victory was no less sweet. The Giants had their first NFL championship since 1938.

After two more successful seasons with the Giants, Vince Lombardi reached his goal. He became a head coach. On February 2, 1959, he signed a five-year contract as coach and general manager of the Green Bay Packers. Vince could hardly wait to tackle the biggest challenge of his life.

7. New Deal at Green Bay

Vince moved his family to Green Bay, Wisconsin, and went to work. Green Bay was a small but thriving city on the western shores of Lake Michigan. It was known for its packing industry, and that's why Green Bay pro teams were known as the Packers.

A coach named Earl "Curly" Lambeau had started the club in 1919. Two years later it joined the National Football League. Lambeau had many fine teams. But when he retired in 1949, the Packers began to slip. In 1958 they won only one game, tied another, and finished last in the league.

The fans were angry. The people of Green Bay really loved football. NFL officials once decided a city of 63,000 was too small to support a big-league team. The townspeople promptly bought enough stock in the club to keep it in the city. All other business stopped when the Packers played at home because everyone was in the stadium. Now many people were losing interest in the team, and fans were demanding a winner.

Vince charged into battle enthusiastically. He tried to rally Green Bay fans behind their club once more. He met the press and talked at civic club meetings.

Some folks still grumbled. "Who is Lombardi?" they asked. He'd been a high school coach, only an assistant in college and with the Giants. "What makes him think he can coach a bunch of losers to victory?"

They soon found out.

The first day of practice Vince walked

into the Packers' dressing room. His eyes gleamed behind his glasses, and his chin was thrust out. The players stared at him coldly as he held up a football.

"This is a football!" he shouted. "Before we're through we're going to ram it down everybody's throat!"

The Packers were dumbfounded. It took real nerve for a new coach to talk to a bunch of veterans like that.

"We're going to be winners," Lombardi announced. "That means hustle. Everybody must be dressed and on the practice field when I blow my whistle. Anyone who's late gets fined."

Vince posted new training rules. Players who loafed in practice or broke the 11:00 P.M. curfew were fined. Those who rebelled were traded or released.

After the second day's practice, Vince found the training room filled with players being treated for minor ailments. "What is this—a hospital?" he roared. "You're supposed to be pros! If you can't play with small hurts you don't belong here!"

The next day when Vince looked in he found only two athletes. As soon as they saw him, they hurried out of the room.

Paul Hornung, a handsome, blond former All-American quarterback at Notre Dame, had been a Packer for two seasons when Vince Lombardi became head coach. And he had been the 1956 Heisman Trophy winner.

When Green Bay drafted him, the fans expected great things. But Paul had played so poorly at quarterback he'd been benched. After that, he'd been moved from one backfield position to another. He was unhappy, and he wanted to be traded.

Even when he heard that Lombardi was the Packers' new head coach, he wasn't impressed. He didn't know that Vince already

Workout time with Vince and the Packers

had watched him on film. Vince didn't like the Packers' performance on that film until he saw Hornung run a play at halfback. Paul ran with such power that he simply bowled the tackler over.

Vince waited impatiently for Hornung to report for practice. When he arrived late, Vince greeted him crisply. "Where've you been?" he asked. Without waiting for a reply he said, "You're my left halfback. You make it there, or you don't!"

Hornung grinned. "Sure, coach," he replied. Paul was as happy as Gifford had been to have a position of his own. Vince now had picked one of his two key players for the Packer offense. The other was Jimmy Taylor, a rookie fullback in 1958.

Lombardi saw that Taylor was a perfect fullback type with his powerful driving legs and hard-muscled body.

"Jimmy—Jimmy!" he'd roar. "Stay with

your blockers! Let them open the hole! Drive past the tacklers—not through them!"

Lombardi soon found blockers for Hornung and Taylor. They were guards Jerry Kramer and "Fuzzy" Thurston, center Jim Ringo, and Forrest Gregg at tackle.

Vince shouted at his players so much he lost his voice for a week. Still he croaked at them, "Block—tackle—that's what it takes to win!"

Some of them resented this hard training. One big lineman said, "Coach is fair, all right. He treats us all the same—like dogs!"

Still they caught Vince's fire—they wanted to be winners. They knew that Vince Lombardi would settle for nothing less.

The quarterback spot was another problem Lombardi faced. He had Lamar McHan, a dependable veteran, and a discouraged holdover named Bart Starr.

Starr didn't help himself with Lombardi

when his first pass in scrimmage was intercepted. "One more like that and you're gone!" Vince bellowed. But Starr fought down his resentment and tried harder than ever.

Before the first pre-season contest, Vince called upon each of his quarterbacks to outline the kind of plays they would call.

Bart surprised the coach. His game outline showed how well he had listened to Vince's chalk talks. "You have a good head on your shoulders," Vince told Bart. "But you must learn to be more aggressive. A quarterback has to be a leader."

McHan started at quarterback when the Packers met the Chicago Bears in their first game under Vince. The Bears led 6–0 at the half. Then Taylor exploded for a touchdown. Hornung kicked the extra point, and a safety added two more as the Packers won 9–6.

The happy Packers boosted Vince on their shoulders. As they paraded around the field, Vince grinned broadly and waved at the cheering fans. "We're on our way!" he shouted.

Vince was right. The Packers won three games in a row. Then McHan was injured.

"All right, Starr," said Vince. "Let's see what you can do."

Bart showed him. Green Bay won its last four games.

The Packers finished third in the West with a 7–5 record. Vince was chosen NFL "Coach of the Year." He had taken a group of losers and made them into a respectable team. "Lombardi did a remarkable job," one reporter wrote. "He turned the Packers completely around."

Vince smiled, but he knew there was room for improvement. Already he was making plans for 1960.

8. "Vince Made Boys into Men"

During Vince's first two years at Green Bay, he drove his team hard to perfect its offense. He built the pass-option play and the power sweep into a two-pronged attack.

He drilled Paul Hornung constantly on the pass-option. "That's it, Paul!" he'd cry as Hornung raced wide. "Now cut in! Pick up your blockers downfield! Run!"

Again he'd yell, "Why didn't you throw? You had two receivers wide open. Wake up, Hornung!"

Vince made sure the blond halfback had good blocking. He sent guards Fuzzy

Thurston and Jerry Kramer to lead the way. He tried to make his blockers proud of their ability.

"You never threw a harder block, Kramer—that's the way!" he'd shout encouragingly. Again, he'd roar, "Don't push that linebacker, Fuzzy! Knock him down!"

Vince worked magic on rejects from other clubs as well as his own veterans. Fuzzy Thurston had been discarded four times when he reached Green Bay.

Thurston was heavily bandaged when he reported for early drills. One day Vince met him at the sideline. "Fuzzy," he said, "if you don't play today, you're through. I'm tired of your complaining." He turned and walked away.

The chunky guard ripped off his bandages. "I'll show that smart guy!" he exclaimed. When he got into scrimmage Fuzzy blocked like a wild man.

The Packers opened the 1960 season against Chicago with Starr at quarterback. They lost 17–14. Vince started McHan again. "Work on your passing," he told Bart. "You need better timing."

Against Baltimore, McHan failed to move the team. "Get in there and start throwing, Starr," ordered Vince. "You can do it!"

Bart did. He outpassed and outgeneraled Johnny Unitas to give the Packers an upset victory. Vince met him at the sideline. "You're number one from now on, Bart," he said.

With Starr guiding the team and Hornung and Taylor racing for touchdowns, the Packers took the Western Division title. It was Green Bay's first division crown since 1944.

In the dressing room after the game, they banged their lockers wildly. Then Vince walked in. "Save that for next week!"

71

he shouted over the din. "We've still got to beat Philadelphia for the league championship!"

Before the game with the Eagles, Vince told the Packers, "We can beat them if we keep rushing. Never let up!"

The Packers drove hard but were held to two early field goals. The Eagles scored a touchdown and a placekick to lead 10–6.

Vince kept urging, "Come on, Packers! Hit 'em—knock 'em down!"

But the Eagles fought back even harder in the second half. After Hornung left the game with injuries, Taylor drove to the seven-yard line. Then Bart fooled the defense. He shot a scoring pass to Max McGee. The Packers led again 13–10.

Philadelphia bounced back with a scoring pass to regain the lead 17–13. The Packers took the kickoff and charged to the Eagles' 22. Time was running out.

Starr cocked his arm and threw. Taylor caught his pass on the nine. Instantly Chuck Bednarik, the Eagles' great linebacker, pinned him to the turf until the final gun.

The loss was a bitter blow to Lombardi. More than anything else in the world, he hated to lose. When reporters questioned him afterward, he was impatient with them.

"What happened, Vince?" one newsman asked.

The core of the Packer team (left to right): Jim Taylor, Lombardi, Paul Hornung, and quarterback Bart Starr.

"You saw the game, didn't you?" replied Lombardi. "They outscored us."

Vince was seldom at ease with writers after a game. He wanted to be with his players. Many writers thought he should be more friendly. They wrote unkind stories about him.

During 1961 training camp, he became even more of a tyrant. He never allowed the Packers to forget that loss to the Eagles. "Your own mistakes beat you!" he'd remind them. "The way you're playing now, the same thing will happen again."

Once during a blocking drill, Jim Taylor was the runner. A huge rookie tackle was blocking for him against defensive back Ray Nitschke. On the first play Taylor slid past Nitschke easily.

Lombardi's whistle blasted furiously. "Mr. Nitschke," he called in a withering tone, "somewhere I read that you are the best linebacker in football. This I find hard to believe. Run it over."

Nitschke did not reply. But this time he seized the big lineman and hurled him into Taylor, knocking them both down.

"Next play," said Lombardi.

After all that rugged training, the Packers lost their NFL opener to Detroit, 17–13.

Vince didn't needle the Packers this time. He didn't have to. They tore into their next two opponents, San Francisco and the Chicago Bears, for one-sided victories.

Hornung stung the Baltimore Colts for 33 points, a new Packer game record. Taylor's turn came against Cleveland. The game was billed as a fullback duel with Jimmy Brown. It was no contest. Taylor scored four touchdowns to completely outclass his rival. Vince began to feel good about the team again.

The Packers stretched their winning streak to six games with a pair of wins over Minnesota. But at this point they ran into a series of setbacks.

They lost Jerry Kramer, star blocking guard, for the season with a broken ankle, and Ray Nitschke was recalled to army duty. He received a pass to play against Baltimore, but he had no time to practice and Johnny Unitas led the Colts to victory.

Then Paul Hornung, too, left for army duty. "Losing these key players hurt," said Lombardi, "but my boys are used to overcoming adversity."

Once again they won the Western Division title, and Vince had his second chance at the NFL crown. The Packers would face New York in the final.

Vince was worried. His team would be playing for the national championship without three top players. He knew the Giants would key on Taylor. Jimmy's rushes had beaten them before.

The army came to the rescue. Hornung was given a week's leave, and Nitschke got a weekend pass. Vince called his veterans together.

"You've come a long way since 1958," he reminded them. "The people of Green Bay have great faith in you. We can't let them down."

Lombardi changed his strategy. "The Giants will be keying on Jimmy," he said. "We'll fool 'em by hitting them outside with Paul."

Before the game Vince saw Starr was pale and nervous. He threw an arm around Bart's shoulders.

"Don't worry, Bart. I know you can do it," he said.

Vince grinned as he saw the Giants mass to stop Taylor. Jimmy faked into the line, and Hornung raced wide for long gains. The Packers led 24–0 at the half.

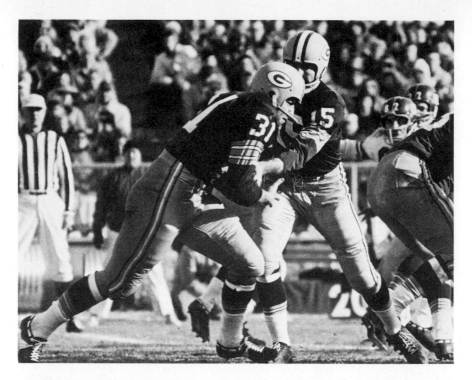

Aided by the quick teamwork of Starr (15) and Taylor (31), the Packers defeat New York and carry Vince off the field in triumph.

"Don't change a thing!" Vince told Starr in the dressing room. "You're doing fine!"

Hornung made 19 points for an NFL scoring record in a championship game. Starr pitched two touchdown strikes, and Nitschke intercepted a pass that led to another. The final score was 37–0, and Vince had his first league title.

That night Vince held a victory party. "Coach had a big smile on his face all evening," one player said. "He kept patting everyone on the back."

"This team's the greatest," said Vince. "There'll never be a better one."

Center Jim Ringo shook his head. "What a change between today and 1958. Vince made that difference. He made a lot of boys into men!"

9. Green Bay Marches On

"Detroit will be tough—even tougher than last time!" Vince Lombardi warned his Packers. It was the week of their Thanksgiving Day game with the Lions in Detroit, November 22, 1962.

The Packers knew what he meant. It had taken Paul Hornung's third field goal in the last 33 seconds to beat the Lions earlier.

Vince knew the pressure would be terrific. Green Bay was riding an eleven-game winning streak. But the Lions were big and tough, and they wanted revenge.

The fired-up Detroiters shocked the Packers from the start. Their huge defensive line stopped Bart Starr eight times in the first half alone. The Lions led 23–0 at halftime.

"You've got to charge quicker!" Lombardi told the linemen in the dressing room. "They're beating you to the punch. Nobody pushes a Green Bay team around like that!"

The Packers came back with one touchdown on an intercepted pass. Jimmy Taylor powered across for another. But the Lions kept right on driving to a 26-14 upset.

Vince spoke quietly to his players after the game. "The real glory is being knocked to your knees and coming up again," he said. "We're no better than anyone else unless we're ready."

"We'll come back," Vince told reporters. "I take the blame for the loss. We changed our defense, and it left the middle wide open. Detroit's line was awfully quick."

The Packers did come back. They finished

the season with a 13–1 record and a third straight Western Division title. That brought them into the 1962 NFL play-off.

Once more they faced New York, this time in frozen Yankee Stadium. The temperature was fifteen degrees above at game time. The wind roared through the stadium.

"Watch out for fumbles," Vince warned. "Everybody's fingers will be numb today." He turned to Starr. "Stick to running plays. Don't try throwing in this wind."

Taylor "runs to daylight" in the 1962 NFL championship game with New York.

The Packers started fast. Hornung and Taylor carried the ball to the New York 26 before the Giants braced.

Then Jerry Kramer, who had replaced Hornung as the placekicker after Paul hurt his knee, kicked the first of three field goals he booted that day. Green Bay led 3–0.

Later the ball slipped from the freezing fingers of a New York halfback. Ray Nitschke swooped down on it like a huge hawk.

Starr promptly called an option pass as the Packers looked at him in surprise. They remembered Vince's instructions.

"That fumble upset them," Starr said briefly. "They won't be expecting a pass."

Hornung ran wide and shot a pass to Boyd Dowler on the Giants' seven. New York massed to stop Taylor. Jimmy crashed straight ahead behind Kramer and Thurston.

The referee's arms shot up. Touchdown!

It was Jimmy's 20th of the season for a new NFL scoring record.

But Taylor paid dearly for his battering charges. Early in the game he bit his tongue so hard it bled. Sick from swallowing blood, Jimmy never stopped driving.

During a timeout he stumbled to the sideline where the trainer wiped the blood from his mouth. Vince bent over him. "How about it, Jimmy?" he asked. "Can you go on?"

Taylor merely nodded and started back to the huddle. Later he told a friend, "You don't know how much you can stand. You think you can't take any more. Then coach steps in and pushes you past that point."

"That was as fine a football game as I've ever seen," Vince told newsmen as Green Bay won 16–7.

"How about Starr's pass to set up that touchdown?" asked someone. "Wasn't that a gamble in this wind?"

"Maybe so," said Vince, "but Bart knew what he was doing."

Another reporter asked, "Think you can make it three straight next year—three titles in a row, coach?"

"What a question!" Vince scoffed. "We'll have to get tougher. We'll have to be even better."

Later Vince spoke to Bill Forester, one of his players, "It's never been done before, Bill."

Forester looked puzzled. "What's never been done before?" he asked.

"Why—winning three NFL championships in a row, of course!"

"But coach," protested Forester, "we've only won two!"

Lombardi's eyes twinkled. "Get with it, Bill. How about next year?"

10. On to the Super Bowl!

For a while it seemed that Vince Lombardi's dream of three straight NFL championships would not come true. There were other strong teams in the league. The Packers finished second in the Western Division the next two years.

Second was never good enough for Vince. He had to have a winner, and he was determined to get it in 1965. "Run!" he'd bellow at a lagging player in practice. "Run if you want to make this team."

The hard training paid off. The 1965

Packers finished the regular season with a 10–3–1 record to face Baltimore in the division play-off.

The game was tied 10–10 at the end of the fourth quarter. Under NFL rules that meant a "sudden death" overtime period. The first team to score would win.

The Packers drove into field-goal position. Don Chandler, their placekicker, was ready. But Bart Starr, who usually held the ball for him, was on the bench. He had been knocked out earlier with injured ribs.

Vince glanced at his quarterback. "Can you do it, Bart?" he asked.

Starr nodded and hobbled out on the field. He placed the ball carefully on the ground. Chandler's kick gave the Packers a 13–10 victory to put them in the NFL play-off against Cleveland.

The Packers faced Cleveland with Starr, Taylor, and Boyd Dowler all heavily taped.

Vince was worried. He seized Ray Nitschke by the arm. "You've got one job to do today!" he told him. "Stop Jimmy Brown!"

The Cleveland fullback was held to 50 yards while Hornung, Taylor, and Chandler led the Packers to a 23–12 victory. As Hornung raced off the field after a touchdown, he shouted, "Just like the good old days!"

Instantly Lombardi was up and shouting, "Hear that, gang? Just like the good old days!"

The "good old days" became even better the next two years.

In 1966 the Packers swept to a 12–2 record, then faced the Dallas Cowboys in the all-league final.

There was an added attraction to the title game. The NFL winner would play in the first Super Bowl game in history. After years of feuding, the NFL and the younger

With the clock running out, Starr (15) scores against Dallas in the 1966 play-off.

American Football League (AFL) had agreed to a championship game.

The Packers took a 14-point lead, but the Cowboys kept fighting back. With five minutes left, the Cowboys trailed 34–27.

The Cowboys hit the Packer two. They were still there on fourth down. "Look out for a pass!" Lombardi shouted. Tom Brown, the Packers' safety man, leaped high to intercept the ball. The Packers had their

90

second straight NFL crown and a chance at the Super Bowl.

Some people called the AFL players "cast-offs" from the older NFL. But not Vince Lombardi. When Frank Gifford, now a TV sportscaster, interviewed him, he said, "We're here to uphold the honor of the NFL—we can't let our league down!"

The Packers met the Kansas City Chiefs in the Super Bowl game in the Los Angeles

Vince closed the triumphant 1966 season with a victory over the Kansas City Chiefs in the first Super Bowl.

Coliseum before 100,000 fans. The Packers won easily, 35–10. "They played like an IBM machine," one reporter said.

Many experts wondered about Green Bay in 1967. Hornung and Taylor were gone. Max McGee and other veterans were aging fast. The Packers did have trouble. They lost nine of fourteen league games. Then they rallied to beat Los Angeles for the division title. Lombardi had done it again.

It would be a repeat from last year—the Packers against the Dallas Cowboys for the NFL championship. A victory would make Vince's dream come true—three straight league crowns for the Packers, plus a second Super Bowl win if they were lucky.

The game between the Packers and the Cowboys was played in Green Bay. The thermometer registered thirteen degrees *below* zero.

Once more Green Bay shot to an early

14–0 lead as Bart Starr pitched two touch-down passes. Again Dallas fought back. With only five minutes left to play Dallas led, 17–14.

Then the Packers marched 68 yards to reach the Cowboys one-yard stripe. Two plays failed. Starr hurried to the sideline to talk to Coach Lombardi.

There were sixteen seconds left. "Shall we go for the touchdown?" asked Starr. "Or should we placekick for a tie—and go into overtime?"

Vince did not hesitate. "Call 31-wedge," he commanded.

Starr nodded. The play called for a perfect block by Jerry Kramer. Behind him would be Bart with the ball.

Kramer hurled his 240 pounds forward at the signal. Daylight flashed between Jerry and tackle Forrest Gregg. Bart charged through it. For an instant the crowd was silent—then a roar went up. Starr had scored the winning touchdown.

Jerry Kramer's block made him one of the game's heroes. Reporters and cameramen crowded around him in the dressing room. Suddenly he raised his hand.

"I'd like to say a word about Coach Lombardi," he said. "A lot has been written about him—some by those who don't understand him. But his players understand him." He pointed at Vince. "Here is one beautiful man!" he shouted.

The Packers won their second Super Bowl game by beating the Oakland Raiders 33–14. Vince's dream had come true—three NFL titles and two Super Bowl championships in a row.

That was Vince's last game as coach of the Green Bay Packers. He retired from coaching in 1968 although he still remained as general manager of the club. But he was

Coach Vince Lombardi—one beautiful man!

restless, and he became coach of the Washington Redskins in 1969.

But the end of Vince Lombardi's fabulous career was already in sight. He became ill with cancer during the season. He died on September 3, 1970.

Great men in many fields paid tribute to him. Perhaps the most fitting words of all, however, were those of Jerry Kramer.

"Here is one beautiful man!"

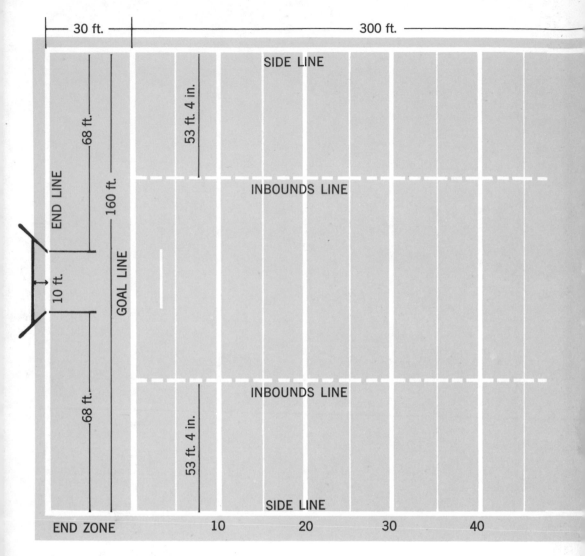

| 30 ft. | 300 ft. |

SIDE LINE

53 ft. 4 in.

END LINE

68 ft.

160 ft.

GOAL LINE

INBOUNDS LINE

10 ft.

INBOUNDS LINE

68 ft.

53 ft. 4 in.

SIDE LINE

END ZONE   10   20   30   40

THE FOOTBALL FIELD

The American Collegiate football field is shaped like a rectangle. It measures 360 feet from one end line to the other, and 160 feet across. The goal lines are 30 feet in from the end lines. The space between the end lines and the goal lines at each end is called the end zone.

In college football, the goalposts are centered on the end lines. The posts stand 23 feet and 4 inches apart and are 20 feet high. The crossbar must be ten feet off the ground. These rules, established in 1958, are slightly different from the rules in professional football.